PERIODS, PAUSES

Periods, Pauses

and other poems

JACQUELINE NICOLE HARRIS

Jacqueline Nicole Harris

I must thank my mom, Sally Ann Harris, who was in every way my hero and the realest woman I've ever known, and my grandmother, Mabel Coburn, for her humble nature & quiet strength. I must thank Judith Kaufman and the Deerfield Library Poets for always encouraging me. I thank God for all my losses and everything I have gained. I want to thank LaToya Howell for letting me into her sorrow.

~Justice for Justus Howell~

~Rest in Peace~

I dedicate this book to my mom and my Godparents, Sherian and "Big" Leo Presley, my uncle JC Coburn and my cousin, Elizabeth Marshall. I miss you all. I hope to see you when I get there.

Periods

By the end of this poem,
I hope you all understand me a little bit better.
I know some of you will be glad when I am finished.
This poem is not an apology, though.
It may sound that way because I spit it so softly.
This poem is not another self-examination
or
another conversation with my inner child.
I have had enough of those talks.
They echo inside my head.
They make me painfully aware of myself
and
conscious when the anguish and pain come out of me.
I still hate the sound of my own voice.
I have *a cry and the world laughs at you* mantra
I repeat to myself from memory
over and over again.
It makes me numb
to the criticism of those
who hear my voice
and
call it dumb
or
read my words
and
call me crazy.
I am not the best poet or wordsmith.
I am not the best anything.
Yet, here I am.
Exposed.

Bare-boned.
Ugly.
Unashamed.
Unabridged.
And
I shall remain unmoved.
And damn you if you think your criticism, your noise,
your indifference stifles my ink.
My life is full of periods, pauses, and breaks just like this poem.
And by the end, I hope you understand
this poem is only another beginning.

Write Happy

                                                                  Cheer up.
                                                                    Smile!

Write about painting rainbows
on white picket fences
in gentrified neighborhoods,

Riding unicorns to Zimbabwe,

Swimming with mermaids in Flint, Michigan waters.

Or

Just sing--
let the wind carry your notes.

Just remember.
                                                             Write happy.

If that doesn't work,
try wearing something nice
and ethnic when you read the poem.

Wear your hair natural in an updo,
with large bamboo earrings.
                                                                  Smile.
No one will question your depth.

                                                            Write happy.

                                                                  Smile!
-not like that!

                                                -like this.
You wore your outfit all wrong.

Smile anyway.

They may laugh,
but it will be at your poem
and (surely) not at you.

If you tried being happy,
maybe someone would understand your poetry.
                                                Smile!
Don't use too many big words.
                                                Write happy.
Try to rhyme.

Aren't you a poet?
                                        Aren't you a Black poet?
Don't you want to be seen?

Don't you want to be loved?
                                                Smile!
Isn't this fun?
                                        Aren't you happy?
Write something happy then.

Write the happy things,
ink the happy thoughts.
Fake it until you make it.
Fake it until you matter.
After all,
this is just performance art.

Blackness & The Palate of the Human Tongue

The human tongue can be divided into 4 areas of taste:
sweet, salty, sour, bitter.
As a black child I went through 4 stages of life before becoming an adult:
Sweet, Salty, Sour, Bitter.

Sweet.

Sweet is innocence.
Sweet is baby steps over cold stones.
Sugary and Saccharine, sweet is when
somewhere, someone draws lines
around you with the sands of time.
Structuring you, defining you like
black plays with black,
stay in your world
with pig tails, and Double Dutch for girls.
Footballs and cap guns for boys.
For example, in the 1980s
during summertime we could play all day
until the streetlights came on.
We were the caramel coated topping
in black suburban life.

Salty.

Salt seeps its way into the blood;
adds savor to the sweet.
Enhances it.
Salty signals change.
Maturation.
Bosom blossoming,

filling out, plumping up
brown sugary sweet
with subtle hints of noticing boys,
who in turn notice you.

Sour.

It all turns to dung.
Sour is a harsh stage where
boys will always be boys if they choose to be
and the title of Lady must be earned if she wants it bad enough.
Sour kills the sweetness of youth.
Sour is when you realize
the hedges of protection around you
were walls that held you inside them.
Walls that say:
This far, no further.
That is not for you.
That was never for you.
Stay Back. Stay here. Stay Black.
WAKE UP!

Bitter.

Bitter is
the real flavor of the design,
don't get it twisted.
Bitter is all that is left
when the youth stay
between the lines.
It is a harsh flavor.
Lingers on the tongue
long after the meal

is finished
and struggles to find
its way down our throats.
Long after the dreams
of youth have lost their sweetness
and the salt and sour
of our experiences have lost their savor—
I ask,
what is left but bitterness and regret with
dead bodies and dreams deferred?

The palette of Black American life
for me has been filled
with so much bitterness
that somedays
I can barely savor
the salt of kind folks
or recognize the sweet.

Somedays,
the milk of human kindness
has soured in me.
And that is frightening,
but if I squint,
I can see the lines
begin to blur,
and remember the lush fullness
of my youth,
my own sweet innocence,
and the flavor of my experiences.

Preoccupied

I am on a park bench,
Sunset Road,
Highland Park, IL.
a mere 30 minutes from the familiar.
My ink is stifled by all the serenity.
The air is clean.
Children play nearby without swearing.
People are walking their dogs
in the emerald green grass.
The trees are lush and ample.
The dogs do their business.
The owners pick it up.
Nearby,
a white woman eyes me suspiciously,
as I watch the children under her charge play in the sun
on a jungle gym shaped like a rocket ship.
I imagine its boosters aflame as I sit in the cooling shade.
It is then I remember, to the north Kenosha, WI is burning.
I remember that while Breonna Taylor is still dead,
Jacob Blake is paralyzed in intensive care.
No one has been charged for killing her;
no one has been charged for shooting him.
The ongoing replays of American grief
are seared deep into my soul while
the sun burns high over the trees in Sunset Park.

Coping in the Light of Corona

Before Corona,
I coped with
the idea of my autonomy.
Now, my daily meditations
turn into short naps.
At the grocery store,
I stared at a stranger
long enough to start
a muffled conversation
over frozen peas.
Though short and sweet,
it was the first real human connection
I'd had in months.
At home, I cook, I eat, I cope
with the new normalcy of pandemic
living, watching the news
reiterate and repeat the collective woes
of a discontented world while wondering--
If we are all in this together,
why do I feel so alone?
Somedays, the quiet becomes unbearable.
But then, sudden sounds cut like a knife.
The phone rings, and
I let telemarketers
talk just to hear the melody
of their breath before
abruptly hanging up on them.
Merely existing is such a burden.
All the while, I wonder:
Can I wash my hands of death?
Is it just inevitable?

Will life go on anyway?
Should I be praying for more time?

And I think . . .

What if life
is all
just one big,
bad
movie
and when
it's over
we die?
All the colors
of life
fade to black
with theme music
blaring
over lists of
rolling credits.
Maybe each
individual
is the star
of their own movie.
The key players
of our lives are there
in the credits.
The ones we loved,
and
the ones we didn't love
mingle with the key grips,
best boys and foley artists
of our lives.
All of them
vying
for credit

in this vast existence.
Maybe
in some other universe
we are the stars
in a never-ending story.
Maybe we are all
sons and daughters of celluloid.
And those who watch us
laugh and cry
because
they feel something.
So,
maybe,
life's not all for nothing.

Of yesterday

I am tired of looking behind,
I want to look forward.
I want to become something,
but I am pulled toward yesterday.
I hate yesterday.
Yesterday is filled with regret,
and horrors that I want to forget.
While today, is fresh air and possibilities.
I crave life like a drug.
And I want to heal.
I know where I've been.
The familiar dread consumes me;
I am sick of it.
There are things I can do,
flavors for me to savor.
Days to dance.
A life to live.
I am not dead yet.
My life is at a standstill.
Somewhere,
sleeping in the earth
of my existence
is what I was meant to become.

Self-Inspection: A poem about my Suicide

If I really believed
that showing off and showing out
could buy me love or raise my self-worth,
I'd rip off my clothes
and rend my naked brown flesh down
to the marrow of my bones--
exposing my soul.
I'd post that shit to YouTube,
and call it trap art.
And with my blood graffitied
all over the walls like a Pollock painting—
I'd probably still be ignored.
The day I tried to kill myself
I reached inside
the deepest part of my being
and told God I hated Him.
I had always imagined that my death,
like prom, would be a house party
that I was never invited too.
It would be a great soiree,
with an amalgam of questions
about the happy coincidence
that was my existence.
But would anyone really care?
I swallowed pills with cough syrup.
I sat on a cold bathroom floor.
I waited on my knees
in darkness with my eyes closed.
I was considerate
enough to unlock the door
but I didn't leave a note.

Meaning to die, never wanting to live—
should have been the epitaph on my tombstone.
I was 21.
Why am I still here?
At 43,
do I still hate God?
No.
I wonder if He hates me, though.
I wonder this
while writing this poem
in a public space
while sipping coffee--
how commercial?
The people around me
are all occupied with each other
as I sit alone, an island of myself.

Postcards and Pictures

Beaming white faces,
dead black bodies.
A severed finger,
a piece of bone,
his genitalia,
her hair--
tokens taken by the hands of persons unknown.
Savor the faded memories,
Lest we forget
the lines drawn in the sand with our blood.

YOUNG MAN
(for Justus Howell)

Young man
I've been waiting for you.
Young Man
I've been anticipating you.
I want to speak to who you are now
Remember your mother
Your first teacher
If she was real
She cried for you
In joy and in silence
In sorrow and with loud exaltation
Remember your father
Your standard
If he was real
He led you here to this moment
With pride and sacrifice he guided your steps.
They are the reason I speak to you.
Young man,
Look around you
360 degrees
And see
This world is yours
Black child,
You are not a bad child.
You were created with love.
You are meant for greatness.
And while forces in this world
may paint the melanin in your skin as evil,
I see the light.
I see your royalty.

I see you.
Young man,
You are potential in motion,
A force of nature.
And if no one ever told you before
You are not a savage!
You were never meant for a cage.
You are not thug!
It is not criminal you exist.
It is not by a whim you are here.
The traps that work against you,
your nature and your purpose
are not mere happenstance.
These things
do not define you!
Tell Satan to get behind you!
Push them away!
Son!
You are a star.
Young man,
You are a king.
Believe it!
Know it!
Stand up.
Stand strong.
Rise with each new day.
Take up the reins of your heart with courage, and live!
One day, young man,
as the sun sets on your life
you will understand.

Oh, Black Woman Sing!

Sing your song. Sing!
With all the harmonies in our triumphs.
With all the lamentations of our souls.
Sing Black Woman!
Sing!
Our foremothers
made melodies from their moans,
found rhythm in their righteous indignation,
found the beauty in their beat,
and kept time on their own.
Your vocals are thunder,
your nature --courage.
You are a well-spring of life anew.
Oh, Black Woman, you must
never be ashamed,
no, never be ashamed of you;
never clothe yourself in silence.
If the act of living is singing a song,
sing life Black Woman!
Sing your defiance!
Sing joy! Sing love! Sing sorrow!
Sing to us our shame!
Sing birth! Sing death! Sing resurrection!
Sing! There is power in your pain.
Sing woman, sing child,
Sing it loud!
Whether Plum dark or faerie Brown.
Sing your song, sing our song.
Oh, Black Woman, sing it!
Sing it proud!

I Still Believe

Call me foolish
if you want to, but
I still believe in miracles,
like I still believe in you.
We are miracles.
I still believe that's true.
Though the devil
may still have
one or two tricks
up his sleeve,
and time has run out for us
to sleep on our dreams,
(Oh yeah)
I still believe.
Hood-raised
men and women
of all shades,
I still believe,
somewhere is a way out
of this motherfucker
for you and me
that don't involve
gentrification,
selling out,
the edge of a razor
or a bullet from a gun.
I still believe.
I believe that
each one
can
teach one.

Like, I still believe
in ink and paper
and its power to reach one.
Oh yeah,
I still believe.
I still believe in reparations
like karma and payback.
I still believe
in the popular vote,
freedom of speech
and proper representation before I'm taxed.
And
I still believe
Heaven's got a hood,
and in black power
and black love
and all of that.
Though others may use
these trying times to wild out
because their shit's confused—
Call me liar, call me a fool.
Call me crazy, call me stupid—
Call this poem fake news.
Black man you are a miracle
and I still believe in you.

Holding on

I hold on to some things longer than others:
anger
love
hate
happiness.
If I think hard,
I might laugh at a joke
I heard in springtime when I was 5.
If I listen to certain songs,
I might remember a bitter moment
and shed ugly tears as fresh as yesterday.
But I don't make a sound
I don't release a peep.
I swallow.
It is all held in me.
I can barely conjure reasons for this.
But I can't help but think
that if I let all of it go,
What will I have?

Issues

Alone.
Wandering hallways of the school if the nurse was absent.
Alone.
Crying in the bathroom like a wolf howling at the moon.
Alone.
Face pocked with acne, feeling gross, unattractive, and more abnormal than usual.
I felt horrible.
I had nothing to count on, no real certainty in my life, except pain and blood.
Sometimes a 10-day stretch, just pain and blood.
It made a stone.
I didn't know about fibroid tumors, or anemia, until later in life.
I suffered so long in silence, I forgot to speak up.
I write this to say, you are normal.
I write this to say if you bleed, then you are normal.
If you feel pain when you bleed, then you are alive.
Pain is real and that is normal.
And if you bleed for 5 days (or more)
a month without dying,
you are blessed.

3 lessons on love

I heard one say *to find love, one must be open to fall in it.*
Well,
I left myself open,
and I fell in;
I am bleeding out now
hoping that
with each
breath I take someone will come
and warm their hands
on the fire of my life's blood.
That sounds a little dramatic.
It was meant to.
Love isn't gentle.
Love is a heavy-handed single mother
braiding
her little girl's tender head
ever so tightly
while the child
jerks and screams
in her lap.
It hurts.
That was the first lesson.
It always hurts.
It's not as soft as red rose petals.
Love is more like pouring
lemon juice
on a thousand paper cuts;
it is relentless.
The second lesson:
you get up
every day alone,

not looking anymore
but looking,
wanting but not needing,
hitting the mark
but missing the target.
And
that X
might mark the spot
that is the one,
but the target,
the find,
the point,
is always love.
This is not about a person,
or implying fault to anyone.
There is no fault in love.
That was my third lesson.
For example,
he never apologized
for hiding a child
from me
while we
were in love.
Lies by omission aren't lies. Right?
Then, why am I still angry?
I left myself open to life
and the lessons of love,
and falling in love,
and
the tried-and-true cliché of being
in love
and the fact is— I loved.

I loved so much that I lost myself. I nurtured the hate that the lies of that love planted within me.

I can't even say it without shame.

I loved him.

And look at what it got me:

a spectacular sense of irony, a biting sarcastic wit, no dignity, and nothing else to lose. Then--

I guess I'll just fall in love with myself.

So, someone asked a question . . .

I heard someone ask
if I were a conscious poet,
and I thought to myself
Pssh! I don't write this shit in my sleep!
Forgive me Lord, I was young and sophomoric.
To me, consciousness
in its infancy
is just a baby
coming out
of its mother's womb
all chubby and slick,
kicking and screaming,
flailing and failing
to comprehend the realness
of the world around them.
I was just like that.
I didn't know shit.
I needed to grow up.
So, I found my ass, and I grew.
Now, I poet,
performance artist,
am a purveyor of thoughts and ideas.
And I don't play
or rather
I take this shit
too seriously
to play by the unspoken rules
of so-called civilized Blackness and poetry.
So,
even in polite company,
my poetry ain't polite.

But, here at home
I am told that I sound too white.
Like
I am weaving bars
and nursery rhymes
to the tune of mother goose.
Like I am sleeping on revolution.
Like I am skimping on all of you.
Well, I have a declaration.
I am conscious,
painfully aware,
Black,
darkly packed,
with pimpled skin,
hair weaved into my naps.
And I say this
without reservation
because I embrace
all my imperfections.
To the beat of my own war drum,
I will march in my own direction,
never mind how I say choice words
with the proper inflection—
My brotha, I know me,
and sista, I love me.
And the pain I rise with daily
just serves to remind me—
I'm woke.
What the fuck do you mean, *am I conscious*?
Inwardly, I laugh at some you—
Calling yourselves Gods
on stage when it's the Most High
who sees your dirt in secret and still allows you to—

Bless His Name!
I bite my tongue
and hold my ink back when I see you.
Because,
on that petty tip,
I could write volumes of BS about you.
But it wouldn't all be BS; it would be true.
But that's not who I am, that's not what I do.
So, sleep on me. I see you.
I heard someone ask if I were a conscious poet,
and I hope you like my answer.
Now that you know it.

Hello reader,

Right now, it is August 29th 2021. My mother passed away in March. I am more burdened down than I have ever been. This may be my last book of poetry (for a while). I feel jaded and honestly tired. But mostly I am sadden by the loss of my mother Sally Ann and by other recent losses. Recently my cousin Monica Goode, passed away.
    I didn't get to go to her homegoing like I wanted. However, my last words to her on her last day were I love you. The same three words I did not get to say to my own mother. My heart breaks every time I think of them. But, to be out of the body is to be in the presence of GOD. My mother would often say many sayings over the years. The one that has stuck the most through these trying times is give people their flowers, while they are living. Don't wait to shower them with roses, when they are gone.

    They don't suffer anymore, and I thank GOD for that.   They lived full lives.
    I hope my mother is proud of me. That's all I ever wanted.

    I hope you have enjoyed my words reader.   I hope to one day bring you more.   Until then, stay tuned.

    Author Jacqueline Nicole Harris

www.ingramcontent.com/pod-product-compliance
Lightning Source LLC
Chambersburg PA
CBHW051215290426
44109CB00021B/2468